Codependent For Sure!

CODEPENDENT

FOR SURE!

by Jann Mitchell

Featuring cartoons by Jennifer Berman,
Joe Spooner, and M.J. Venezky

Andrews and McMeel
A Universal Press Syndicate Company
Kansas City

Design by Rick Cusick

Cartoons appearing on pages 11, 27, 36, 47, 67, and 81, copyright © 1992 by Jennifer Berman.

Library of Congress Cataloging-in-Publication Data

Mitchell, Jann.
    Codependent for sure! / by Jann Mitchell ; featuring cartoons by Jennifer Berman, Joe Spooner, M.J. Venezky.
      p. cm.
    ISBN 0-8362-7998-0 : $6.95
    1. Codependency—Humor. 2. Codependents—Humor. I. Spooner, Joe.
II. Venezky, M.J. III. Title.
PN6231.C563M57 1992
818'.5402—dc20   92-14541
                                                          CIP

Attention: Schools and Businesses

Andrews and McMeel books are available at quantity discounts with bulk purchase for educational, business, or sales promotional use. For information, write to: Special Sales Department, Andrews and McMeel, 4900 Main Street, Kansas City, Missouri 64112.

For Ted, who spurred me
   toward recovery;
for Sheri and Bonnie,
   who set me on the path;
and for the Tuesday noon "kids"
   who kept me company.

Contents

Introduction

As a newspaper feature writer and relationship columnist, I have stacks of self-help books sprouting from my desk like stalagmites. Occasionally, they are knocked over by intense authors gesturing during interviews.

One day as I picked up a pile of toppled titles, it occurred to me: Why does recovery have to be so grim?

What we in recovery needed, it seemed to me, wasn't yet another how-to book, what we needed was a good laugh. We've been working so hard at recovery from our assorted addictions, compulsions, and codependency, that we deserved a break—sort of an adult recess.

I began making codependent cracks, and my recovering friends laughed in recognition—just as we had cried together and nodded in relief that we weren't crazy and we weren't alone.

Lord knows we had enough to laugh at. Once past the pain, it looked so ludicrous: the midnight drive-bys, the crazy attempts to control everything and everybody, the Keystone Kops comedy routines we enacted to outrun our fears.

Ever notice how in the movies, after a big scare or good cry, a gut-busting laugh occurs soon after? It's called comic relief. Laughter discharges pent-up tension. And laughing at ourselves provides respite from the pain.

It also acts as a mirror; if we can see the folly of a cartoon character's actions and beliefs, then we can cut through our denial and rationalization. When we · see ourselves and laugh, we're acknowledging the truth. Even scientists are recognizing the healing powers of humor.

Some of us family mascots and class clowns have used comedy to medicate our pain; we used laughter as a lozenge. That's not good. We have to uncover the cause of codependency, not just salve the symptoms. That's different from using humor to heal.

In codependency recovery, we learn that if we can feel it, then we can heal it. And if we have healed it, then we can afford to lighten up. This book isn't to shame us for our behavior; it's to help us smile at our behavior.

So where do I get so many codependent gags? Easy. I open my journal, close my eyes and point. Even slips aren't relapse, they're research. Sort of a cartoon version of "This Is Your Life."

I'll bet it was your life, too. But we've got the last laugh now.

—*Jann Mitchell*

Some experts say that when we go to work, we simply shift our dysfunctional family roles to the workplace. Finding a normal boss is about as easy as finding normal parents. Although my boss is lots nicer than my relatives! He hardly ever hits us. Just the other day, I went into his office and said, "How about a raise, Dad . . . er, Mr. Quigley?" He said no, but he did give me his cigar band to wear as a ring. Nobody else in the office got one. I think I'm his favorite.

I love my job—I just can't get enough of it. This place

would fall apart without me. Some days I feel I'm going to fall apart instead, but I hang on just knowing that someday Mr. Quigley will appreciate me.

. . . Before I retire, I hope.

Codependent Thought for the Day:

Codependents are people of conviction—
after they find out what everyone else thinks.

Then there was the codependent
stockbroker who got fired—

He only felt needed when the market fell.

Codependent Dream Jobs

AIR TRAFFIC CONTROLLER: Hold the fates of thousands in your hands daily—ultimate control. Stress guaranteed.

MINDREADER: Put your natural skills to work and predict the future for others. Easy money; crystal ball provided.

HOUSEKEEPER: Compulsive cleaner wanted.

Why did the codependent's office look like a landfill?

Because he let everyone dump on him.

~ THE CODEPENDENT HANDSHAKE ~

~ RETIRED CODEPENDENTS ~

The Codependent Briefcase

Codependent Hotline

"You have reached the Codependent Hotline.

"If you want to save the world, press 1.

"If you want to rescue your family, press 2.

"If you want to change your partner, press 3.

"If no one appreciates you, press 4.

"If you do not have a Touch Tone phone, stay on the line and an operator will speak with you after she's through with the really important people."

Codependent Bumper Stickers

23

Q: *What do you call a codependent who says "no" and doesn't feel guilty?*

A: Healthy.

Hey, who says codependency isn't cool? We've got more books written about us now than yuppies do . . .

Maybe that's because we're not selfish like they are. No-sir-ee, we've got better things to do than make our own pasta. We've got the world to save.

We've got more important things to worry about than what color upholstery we want in our BMWs—like world hunger, the ozone layer, and whether or not complete strangers like us.

And we meet so many interesting people. People who wouldn't be doing life or be on death row if they only had someone like us to really understand them. It's just amazing how many people need our advice—even if they don't always take it.

Sometimes I wonder if there's not more to life, though. Maybe we would be happier if we had BMWs with red leather seats.

You're codependent for sure if, when you die, someone else's life flashes in front of your eyes.

The Codependent Salute

31

You're codependent for sure when you get kicked off jury duty for insisting that you're the guilty one.

Q. Why did the codependent cross the road?
A. To help the chicken make a decision.

33

Codependent Cosmetics

OBSESSION *Cologne*

COMPULSION *Perfume*

STRONG AND SILENT *Aftershave*

NEVER LET GO *Hair Spray*

RESCUER RED *Lipstick*

PEOPLE PLEASER PINK *Lipstick*

COVERT GIRL *Liquid Make-up*

I *Shadow*

HYDIT *Emotion Lotion*

DON'T GIMMENY *Lip Pencils*

FOOL 'EM *Blemish Concealer*

FIXEM *Deodorant for Others*

BABBLE *Bath*

BANISHING *Cream*

Codependent Thought for the Day:

So many people to rescue,
so little time.

Codependent Thought for the Day:

*You can always tell a codependent—
but you can't tell him much.*

Q: *What's an insomniac dyslexic codependent do at night?*

A: You lie awake trying to figure out why you can't trust in dog.

Q. How many codependents does it take to screw in a lightbulb?
A. Three—one to do it, one to tell her how, and one to go tell the addict that you've done his job for him, again.

39

Did you hear about the codependent who flunked geography?
He couldn't distinguish any boundaries.

Q: *Why do codependents get off so cheap at the hospital?*

A: They require no anesthesia and use only Band-Aids.

Q: *What do you get when you combine a codependent woman with someone with extra-sensory perception?*

A: A know-it-all bitch!

You know you're codependent if you find yourself in
a rut—and move in furniture.

Codependent Insurance:

My fault.

I know this woman who is *really* messed up. Every single meeting or lecture or workshop I go to, there she is!

I used to think, there's just no more good men or women left. Everyone's screwed up, and I've dated them all.

Face it: Love isn't like it is in the movies. Walt Disney and Doris Day lied to us. I want my money back.

Oh sure, I'd hear violins when we'd meet, but when it was time to sing, they never knew the words. People in the movies don't have ex's and stepchildren who pretend you're not in the room. And when movie couples go for marriage counseling, they don't break up in the parking lot afterward.

Maybe real-life love would be more like real-life romance if we ate more popcorn. Just spending time in the dark hasn't helped.

The experts say we're as healthy as our partners. Who wants to look at ourselves? It was so much easier thinking everyone else had a problem.

First codependent couple: Adam and Eve

Eve listened to a snake instead of herself,
and Adam blamed her for all their problems.

Q. What keeps a codependent from being ambidextrous?
A. We have to be right and dread being left.

51

Codependent Thought for the Day:

Behind every successful man is a codependent reminding him how he got that way.

"SURE I DO AFFIRMATIONS. I PRAY AND MEDITATE AND VISUALIZE, TOO. BUT WHEN I REALLY WANT TO FEEL GOOD ABOUT MYSELF, I WEAR MY BLACK PUSH-UP BRA."

53

Codependents are the only people—

who go to marriage counselors by themselves.

Codependents At A Movie

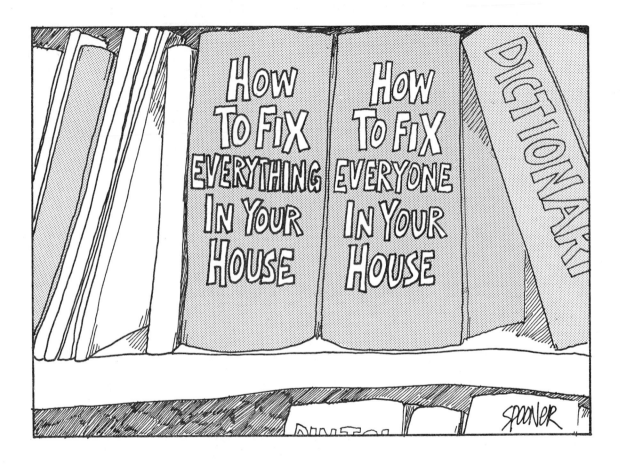

Codependent Handbook

Codependent First Date

7:00 p.m.	You meet at a restaurant, driving your own car so you can leave if you want.
7:25 p.m.	You finish telling your life story.
7:30 p.m.	He finishes his life story.
8:00 p.m.	You feel so close you decide to bag dinner and go back to your place.
8:30 p.m.	This intimacy feels so good, you go to bed together.
9:30 p.m.	You discuss marriage.
11:00 p.m.	He goes home because he has to be in the office early in the morning.
11:30 p.m.	He calls to say he made it home safely.
11:35 p.m.	You begin debating on whether you should move in with him or he should move in with you.
Midnight	You get dressed and drive over to his place to measure his dining room.
12:30 a.m.	You wind up in bed and stay the night.

8:00 a.m.	You go home to change and he follows you in his car so he can take you to work.
9:30 a.m.	You make a lunch date together.
Noon	Over lunch, you discuss moving this weekend.
1:00 p.m.	You extend your lunch hour to shop for an engagement ring.
2:00 p.m.	You show your ring to co-workers, who plan a shower.
5:30 p.m.	You meet for dinner and finally get to eat it.
8:00 p.m.	You go to his place and measure his bedroom.
8:30 p.m.	You make love.
9:30 p.m.	You discover his dog has eaten your best shoes. He says, "So keep your shoes on the dresser." You get mad. He says, "Well, the dog stays, no matter what."
9:45 p.m.	You huff out in tears and take a cab home.
10:15 p.m.	You call and argue for 20 minutes.
11:00 p.m.	He knocks on the door, demanding his ring.
11:05 p.m.	You throw it at him.
11:15 p.m.	You sob a half hour, then write in your journal: Who needs him? And my dining table was too big anyway.

You're codependent for sure when you wake up in the morning and say to your mate:
"Good morning, how am I?"

the CODEPENDENT DATE

61

~ CODEPENDENT JUKEBOX FAVORITES ~

Top Ten Codependent Phrases:

1. *Okay . . .*
2. *If only . . .*
3. *Whatever You Want*
4. *Let Me Help You*
5. *It's Really Not So Bad*
6. *This Time Things Will Be Different*
7. *What Do You Think I Should Do?*
8. *No Thanks, I Can Do It All Myself*
9. *Honey, I'll Be Whatever You Want Me to Be*
10. *I Can't Go into Treatment—Too Many People Need Me*

Codependents don't have relationships—

they have caseloads.

Alice & Ralph Kramden

Archie & Edith Bunker

Cathy & Heathcliff

Rhett & Scarlett

Lucy & Ricky

Ward & June

Romeo & Juliet

Ozzie & Harriet

~ THE CODEPENDENT COUPLES HALL of FAME ~

~ CODEPENDENTS DON'T FALL IN LOVE, THEY TAKE HOSTAGES. ~

Entertainment

Who needs to go out for entertainment?

Codependents are the original VCRs, continually replaying classic movies in our heads. There's The Meeting, The Short-Lived Romance, The Split, The Reunion, The Split, The Reunion—oops, the tape's stuck.

When we do watch a movie, we really think we can change the outcome. Maybe this time Scarlett will talk Rhett into giving a damn. Clap your hands if you believe in fairies or Tinker Bell will surely die.

And soap operas? Who do you think invented them? If we dress our families in designer clothes and change their names from Frieda and Sam to Brittany and Zach, then we might have a good shot at prime time.

All of our great literature comes from the self-help section. And as for music, codependence is just one long country song.

Q: *Why does a codependent buy two copies of every self-help book?*

A: One to read and one to pass on to someone who really needs it.

Codependent Palmistry

Codependent Olympic Events

BLAME TOSSING

SHOTGLASS PUT

DENIAL BIATHLON

LOVERS LUGE

THIN-ICE SKATING

DOWNHILL
   RELATIONSHIP SLALOM

CROSS-COUNTRY SPYING

400-METER REPLAY

UNBALANCED BEAM

OLYMPIC BACKSLIDING

THE PEOPLECHASE

UNEVEN PARALLEL
   BARSEARCHING

~ THE CODEPENDENT VACATION ~

73

Codependent Music to Be Miserable By:

Don't Give Up on Us, Baby
The Things We Do for Love
You Needed Me
Another One Bites the Dust
Do That to Me One More Time

Codependent Calisthenics

You may be screwed up, but you sure are physically fit!

RUNNING: See how fast you can run away. From yourself. From your parents. From your mate. Vary your route to avoid predictable patterns.

SIT-UPS AND PUT-DOWNS: Just the exercise for enabling you to sit there and take it, then shoot back passive-aggressive remarks.

CHIN-UPS: Perfect for developing that chin-held-high pose so no one can see how rotten you feel.

KNEE-JERK: Puts your knees in shape for responding automatically, without thinking.

BENCH PRESS: Develop those shoulder muscles and you'll be able to carry the weight of the world on your back.

Codependent Animal Classics:

Lassie—The Ultimate Rescuer

Mr. Ed—Obsessive Talker

Silver—Lone Ranger's Enabler

Cheetah—The Tarzan Family Mascot

Codependent Soap Operas:

One Louse to Love
Many Others Lives to Live
The Young and the Rescuer
Decades of Our Lives
As the World Turns Around Me
All My Responsibilities
The Guiding Wife

Codependent Travel Guide

ENGLISH: *"To make your country better . . ."*

GERMAN: *"Um ihr land besser zu machen, sollten sie . . ."*

ENGLISH: *"I'm sorry."*

SPANISH: *"Lo siento."*

ENGLISH: *"It doesn't matter to me, whatever you want . . ."*

FRENCH: *"Peu importe. Comme vous voulez . . ."*

It's not that we haven't tried to change our lives.

We've tried drinking, drugging, spending, loving, and eating. We've read books, gone to workshops, and played tapes—both audible and subliminal. We've gotten centered, cleared, enlightened, and self-actualized. We've screamed primally and beaten pillows with foam bats. We've had our families sculptured, our behavior modified, our pasts dissected, and our futures predicted.

We've had our auras read, our chakras opened, our palms peered into, and our colors analyzed. We've been massaged, wrapped, saunaed, floated, and stretched. We've been depilated and debilitated, compressed and depressed. We would have been Rolfed, but he wasn't in.

Then we found recovery—an option we'd postponed. Probably because it requires work.

Codependent Thought for the Day:

Toxic shame is like toxic waste:
Nobody wants to own it.

Q: *What's the difference between a recovering codependent and a pit bull?*

A: Meetings.

Know the difference between a codependent
and a hijacker?

You can argue with the hijacker.

A codependent finally gets up the nerve to go to a therapist:
"You're codependent," the therapist says.
"I demand a second opinion."
"Well, you're ugly, too."

Q: *What does a codependent have in common with God?*

A: They both have a plan for your life.

Did you hear about the codependents who died and went to heaven?
There were two doors—the one on the left was marked "Heaven" and the one on the right "Lecture About Heaven."

Codependent Prayer:

"Lord, Give Me Patience, Now!"

Jann Mitchell is a feature writer and relationship columnist for *The Oregonian* in Portland. She has received national awards for her work on addiction and mental health—including the National Journalism Award from the National Association of Addiction Treatment Providers. She has also won top honors for humor writing from the National Federation of Press Women. She is also the author of *Organized Serenity*.